# Low-carb juices and smoothies

Amanda Cross

hamlyn

# Low-carb juices and smoothies

**50 healthy, delicious recipes**

First published in Great Britain in 2005
by Hamlyn, a division of
Octopus Publishing Group Ltd
2–4 Heron Quays  London  E14 4JP

Distributed in the United States and
Canada by Sterling Publishing Co., Inc.
387 Park Avenue South, New York,
NY 10016-8810

ISBN 0 600 61393 3
EAN 9780600613930

A CIP catalogue record for this book is
available from the British Library

Printed and bound in China

10 9 8 7 6 5 4 3 2 1

# Contents

# Introduction

Low-carb eating is no longer just a dietary fad, taken up by those who want to lose weight quickly, but has become a way of life for people seeking to improve their overall wellbeing. The original ethos of eating high quantities of saturated fats combined with limited fruit and vegetables has been replaced with a far healthier approach.

It is fast becoming generally accepted that in order to combat the rising number of people suffering from degenerative conditions such as diabetes, coronary heart disease, and cancer, it is necessary to reduce refined carbohydrates and fatty "junk" foods from our diet. Eating high-quality protein, complex carbohydrates, and unsaturated fats which are high in essential fatty acids (see page 10) can not only help you lose weight, but will also improve your overall health.

## Extreme dieting

In the past, low-carb diet plans have led to many dieters overreacting by reducing or even cutting out fruit and vegetables from their diets.

According to a report by A. C. Nielsen (a leading market information company) in 2004, it is estimated that roughly 11 million Americans have dropped fruit from their diets as a result of low-carb dieting. In

### Growing popularity of low-carb diets

A 2003 Gallup Poll disclosed that 47 percent of the U.S. population is now monitoring their carbohydrate intake. It is estimated that the "low-carb" diet is now followed by over 50 percent of weight-conscious Americans. The sales of low-carb products and services in 12 months alone have recently been estimated at around $15 billion.

In the U.K. many people are opting for a diet high in protein and healthy fats. The Atkins regime claims to have over 3 million devotees in the U.K.

While low-carb diets have become a celebrity craze and received some bad press, common sense alone dictates that we should be looking at reducing our levels of carbohydrate.

a survey of one thousand Americans, 12 percent said they were on a low-carb diet, 30 percent said they had reduced their fruit consumption, and 14 percent said they had eliminated fruit from their diet completely. Going to such extremes is unadvisable: fruit and vegetables are essential sources of vitamins and minerals that are vital for maintaining a healthy diet.

The U.S.D.A. (United States Department of Agriculture) Food Guide Pyramid recommends eating 2–4 servings of fruit a day and 3–5 portions of vegetables. Fruits and vegetables are excellent sources of vitamins A and C and a host of minerals. However, because many fruits and root vegetables contain carbohydrates, some low-carb diets don't include them except in very limited amounts, particularly in diets aimed at quick weight loss.

## Make the right choices

It is quite possible to enjoy fruits and vegetables while sticking to a low-carb diet. You just have to make the right choices and keep to the fruits and vegetables with the lowest density of carbohydrates. Remember to include them in your daily carb allowance if you are following a specific plan.

Like many things in life, any diet is a matter of common sense and moderation. Too rigid a regime will become boring, whereas a diet that is not sensibly balanced with the full range of nutrients necessary for the normal functioning of the body can lead to nutritional deficiencies and compromised health. Juices can be part of a healthy diet plan and provide vitamins and minerals in an easily assimilated form. Their effect on blood sugar can be controlled by combining them with high-protein snacks.

In order to monitor your carbohydrate intake and ensure that your juices are of the highest nutritional value, it is best to make your own. Use high-quality ingredients and avoid drinking commercially made juices that often contain high-carb sugars and additives.

It's not easy making lifestyle changes, but once you get into a routine, it'll soon become second nature. There are plenty of delicious ingredients that are low in carbohydrates. And not only will you be improving your health, but you could lose weight and improve your self-esteem at the same time.

# Why low carb?

Even though carbohydrates are a vital part of our diet since they are our primary source of energy, many people are eating far too many of the wrong sort of carbohydrates. This is contributing to the worldwide obesity problem and to the growing numbers of people suffering from serious illness related to this.

## What are the bad carbs?

Essentially, there are three main types of carbohydrates:
- **Simple sugars or monosaccharides:** glucose (blood sugar) and fructose (fruit sugar).
- **Double sugars or disaccharides:** lactose (milk sugar).
- **Complex carbohydrates or polysaccharides:** starches and cellulose (potatoes, rice, grains, and dietary fiber).

The bad carbs are the refined carbohydrates such as white flour and sugar that have been stripped of the nutrients which the body requires to metabolize them. Once the refining process has removed magnesium, zinc, chromium, and B vitamins from white flour and sugar, they become not only nutritionally redundant but actually deplete the body of the vital minerals and vitamins that are needed to perform other important bodily functions.

So is it enough just to stop taking white sugar in your coffee?

Unfortunately not. Refined carbohydrates lurk in virtually all junk food along with unhealthy hydrogenated fats, high levels of salt, and a host of additives. These nutritionally empty foods make up 75 percent of many people's diets.

These refined carbohydrates have a detrimental impact on your overall health. They hit the bloodstream very quickly and raise blood sugar (and, as a result, insulin levels). The blood sugar then drops rapidly, causing the body to crave another carb hit. So, if you have ever wondered how you can go back to the biscuit tin again and again and never feel sated, this is why.

## Do you have any of these symptoms?

**Fatigue**

**Mood swings**

**Brain fog and inability to concentrate**

**Carbohydrate cravings**

**Bloating**

**Constant hunger**

**Continual yo-yo dieting**

*Does this all sound a bit familiar?* If so, then there is a good chance you could be a carbohydrate junkie.

It's time to reevaluate your diet, chuck out some bad habits, and embrace a few healthy low-carb lifestyle guidelines.

## If you do, then cut out these foods:

White bread and bread products

White rice

Refined sugar

Salt

Sodas

Bottled cordials and juice drinks

Candy

Chocolate

Margarine

Sweet cookies and cakes

Canned fruit and vegetables (unless they are canned in water)

Processed meat products

Sugar-loaded cereals

Sweetened fruit yogurts

Ice cream (unless you buy a low-carb brand)

White pasta

Prepacked convenience meals

Sauces and gravy mixes

# But what can I eat?

Don't panic, you won't starve! In fact you'll thrive if you eat more of the following:

## High-fiber fruits and vegetables

**Fruits and vegetables** can be added to salads, stir-fried, or steamed as an accompaniment. It is important to include a healthy range in your diet every day, raw if possible.

## Healthy fats

**Cold-pressed unrefined oils** such as olive, sunflower, safflower, corn, flaxseed, and sesame; plenty of oily fish; and nuts and seeds rich in omega-3 and omega-6 fatty acids will keep your body healthy and act as a secondary source of energy.

## High-quality protein

**Fish and shellfish** and especially omega-3 rich oily fish such as sardines, mackerel, tuna, and salmon are an excellent source of protein. Pack your refrigerator with fish and shellfish. Just make sure it's fresh and comes from a reliable source.

**Poultry and game** is a particularly lean and healthy option. Try organic or free-range chicken, turkey, wild duck, pheasant, quail, rabbit, venison, and wild boar.

**Meat** should be organic if possible. Barbecue some beef, lamb, or pork, or jazz up a salad with a little organic bacon and ham.

**Eggs** can be boiled or scrambled and should be organic if possible.

**Cheese** should be eaten in moderation, but the occasional 3 1/2 oz portion of organic cheese is totally acceptable.

**Soy** products are high in healthy protein. If you are vegetarian or just fancy a change, tofu, tempeh, and other soy products are good, low-fat choices.

**Whey protein powder** is a great source of high biological value protein.

# Why juice?

An easy way to hit your five-a-day target of fruit and vegetables is to include low-carb juices and smoothies in your diet. The most important benefit of juicing is the range and quantity of vitamins, minerals, phytonutrients, and enzymes that are present in fruits and vegetables. These are fundamental to optimum health. Phyto-nutrients are compounds in fruits and vegetables that are at the cutting edge of medical research as some believe they hold the key to preventing many degenerative diseases. They detoxify the body, lower blood cholesterol levels, and combat free radicals—the reactive molecules that attack cells and cause premature aging.

Cooking vegetables destroys many of these essential enzymes. Because these enzymes are responsible for maintaining a healthy metabolism, digesting and absorbing food, and converting it into body tissue and producing energy, it is better to consume most of these fruits and vegetables raw. These nutrients are bound to the plant in a form that is assimilated by digestion. Juicing removes the indigestible fiber, releasing the nutrients to the body more quickly and in larger quantities. There are also important nutrients in the pith and seeds of many fruits and vegetables that juicing makes available.

Fruits and vegetables also provide another necessary substance to the human body—water. As many of the beverages of choice for most people—coffee, tea, alcohol, and sodas—tend to dehydrate the body, juices are a great choice.

## Make it colorful

If you don't want to memorize a long list of vitamins, antioxidants, phytochemicals, and minerals, the easiest way to ensure you are getting the best nutritional combination of natural foods in your shopping cart is to make sure it features greens, reds, oranges, yellows, and purples— the more colorful your fruits and vegetables the better. If all you can see in your cart is a pile of cardboard boxes and microwavable food then you are doing something wrong. Because many fibrous green vegetables are lower in carbs than fruits, combining the two works well to lower carbohydrate levels and yet still create a pleasant-tasting juice.

## Protective nutrients

By increasing your intake of low-carbohydrate vegetables in your diet, you will be on your way to becoming much healthier. The nutrients found in raw, organic fruit and vegetables can protect you from ill health in many different ways. In addition, they will keep you feeling full for much longer than "empty" snacks like chips and chocolate. The nutrients give you an energy boost and if you consume them regularly, you will have more energy to face each day. The information below shows some of the benefits to be had.

**Garlic and onions** contain allyl sulphide. This is antiviral, antibacterial, and helps to eliminate toxins from the body.

**Leafy green vegetables, beet tops, and squash** contain lutein. As well as being an antioxidant, this is also antiaging, and promotes good eyesight.

**Cruciferous vegetables such as broccoli and cauliflower and leafy green vegetables** contain indoles and sulforaphanes, which eliminate toxins, boost immunity, and may remove carcinogens from cells.

**Tomatoes, watermelon, pink grapefruit, and strawberries** contain lycopene, P-coumaric acid, and coumarins. All of these are antioxidants, and may reduce the risk of cancer. They also reduce inflammation.

**Citrus fruits** contain limonene and glucarase. These enhance immunity, eliminate degenerative chemicals from the body, and help with production of anticancer enzymes.

**Mangoes, pumpkins, carrots, sweet potatoes, and squash** contain alphacarotene and betacarotene. These potent antioxidants are also immune boosters and may help to prevent aging.

**Berries and red grapes** contain polyphenols and flavonoids which some evidence shows to lower the risk of heart disease, strengthen blood vessels, and flush out dangerous chemicals.

# 6 good reasons to juice

1  Easy assimilation of vital nutrients
2  More nutritious than commercially prepared heat-treated juices
3  Detoxifying and cleansing
4  Quick meal replacements
5  Antiaging
6  Super-body booster properties to aid recovery from illness.

# Will it be sweet enough?

On a low-carb plan it is vital to cut out nutritionally redundant white sugar. However, what if you have a sweet tooth and the natural sweetness of fruits, vegetables, and natural flavorings isn't enough? You then have to make an informed choice about the type of sweetener to use. Regulations vary in different countries and there is continual controversy about one of the most common artificial sweeteners— aspartame. Alternatives include Splenda (made from natural sugar and widely available) and Stevia (a safe natural plant extract that has been used by South American Indians for years and appears to contain many health benefits, ranging from retarding plaque to inhibiting growth of streptococcus and other bacteria).

# Top tips

● When following a low-carb diet, try combining juices with a protein snack such as nuts or seeds. This can also be achieved by adding soya or dairy products such as cottage cheese or yogurt or whey protein powder to a smoothie. This will help to regulate blood sugar levels.

● You can still enjoy high-carb fruit juices if you dilute them with sparkling or still water, or, for an added flavor twist, try them with chilled herb teas and infusions.

● Combine lower-carb vegetables with higher-carb fruits to make tasty lower-carb juices with maximum nutritional impact.

# How to juice

If you are going to incorporate healthy juices and smoothies into your diet, your first step is to equip yourself with the proper appliances. It is worth spending as much as you can afford on good-quality machines of a reputable brand. Cheaper ones may seem like a bargain but all too often they break down quite soon.

You may already have a citrus press, which is fine for extracting juice from citrus fruit, but it is better to use a dedicated juicer as you will benefit from the nutrients contained in the pith and seeds.

## Blender

Look for a blender that has a variety of speeds as you will need to be able to crush ice and blend frozen fruit. Hand-held immersion blenders are not really designed to do this, and, unless you have a very deep container, the liquid will fly everywhere.

## Juicers

There are two main types of juicer. A key point to remember is that the drier the pulp, the more effective the juicer.

### Centrifugal juicer

This is the most affordable and widely used juicer. The fruits and vegetables are fed into a rapidly spinning grater and the juice and pulp are separated. In general a smaller amount of juice is produced than by the larger masticating or pulverizing juicer.

### Masticating juicer

The larger, more expensive juicers usually have a masticating or pulverizing action. The fruits and vegetables are pushed through a wire mesh—this action is very powerful and produces a high level of juice (which is very nutrient-dense) and very dry pulp. As this juice isn't extracted through spinning metal blades, the process avoids overheating and destroying some of those vital enzymes.

# Top tips

- Use fresh and firm fruits and vegetables for the maximum nutrient content.

- Wash all fruits and vegetables thoroughly to remove any dirt or chemicals.

- Remove all stems and large pits.

- Do not force fruits and vegetables into the juicer. Pass them through slowly and steadily using the pusher provided—never use knives or other metal kitchen implements.

- Do not cut fruits and vegetables too small—ideally cut them to a size that fits comfortably into the chute.

- Alternate soft fruits and vegetables with harder ones; this will help push the softer fruits through.

- When juicing leafy vegetables, roll them into a ball and push them through followed by harder fruits or vegetables.

- Don't try to juice bananas, avocados, or overripe fruit—this will clog up the juicer. Use these in smoothies.

- Never juice raw rhubarb or eggplants. They both contain toxic substances that are destroyed during the cooking process.

- The most aggravating aspect of juicing is cleaning the machine. This has to be done immediately you have finished juicing, and you must do it thoroughly as any residue will harbor bacterial growth. For this reason, look for a machine that dismantles easily.

- Most machines come with a special brush to clean the mesh or grater. Wire cleaning pads are excellent for this job. Soaking in warm soapy water can make the task a little easier. If the plastic parts of the machine become stained, use a mixture of one part white vinegar to two parts water to remove the discoloration.

- Rather than throw away the fruit and vegetable pulp, it can be added to smoothies, muffins, soups, casseroles, meat dishes, etc., for added nutrition and fiber. Just collect it in a plastic container, add a little lemon juice, and freeze it until you want to use it.

# Top 10 low-carb fruits

**Apples** are an excellent juicing ingredient. They contain antioxidants, reduce cholesterol, cleanse the digestive system, and boost the immune system. They provide an excellent base for many juices, and even a small quantity of apple will soften the taste of a stronger vegetable blend. Apples are also full of nutrients that aid in the digestion of fats.
**11.8 g carbs per 100 g**

**Avocados** are a complete food, packed with essential nutrients. They lower blood cholesterol and contain glutathione which blocks 30 different carcinogens. The high vitamin E content is excellent for maintaining a healthy skin, wound healing, and, of course, bolstering the immune system. Avocados are also a good source of lecithin, which helps the body digest and metabolize fats. Their consistency is perfect for use in smoothies.
**1.9 g carbs per 100 g**

**Berries** are all valuable low-carb ingredients that do a great deal for our general health so it is difficult to pick one in particular. Even out of season, fill your freezer with nutritious red and purple berries. They are antiviral and antibacterial. Berries of all sorts are good for the bloodstream. Blueberries and black currants help if you have diarrhea or any urinary infection. Raspberries contain natural aspirin (through their antiinflammatory properties) and are reputedly good for menstrual cramps.  Strawberries are high in pectin, full of lycopene, and benefit the cardiovascular system as a whole.
**5–6 g carbs per 100 g**

**Citrus fruits** are another important group of fruits that are difficult to split up. Collectively oranges, lemons, limes, and grapefruits contain carotenoids, bioflavinoids, and huge levels of vitamin C that are key in the fight against cancer. They also lower blood cholesterol and arterial plaque. Citrus fruits are antiviral, antibacterial, and extremely versatile, not least for the great burst of flavor they give any juice or smoothie.
**Oranges 8 g carbs per 100 g; grapefruit 6.5 g per 100 g; lemons and limes 2.5 g per 100 g**

**Cranberries** deodorize urine and inhibit bacteria in the bladder, prostate, and kidneys. They have the power to keep the entire urinary tract free from infection as they contain mannose which is more effective than antibiotics. Cranberries can also help prevent kidney stones and are antiviral and antibiotic. They are very sour and may need to be combined with sweeter fruit when used in juices and smoothies.
**3.5 g carbs per 100 g**

**Kiwi fruits** are packed with vitamin C and are full of fiber. They contain actinidin, an enzyme which is excellent for the immune system, lowering blood pressure, and contributing to general heart health. Kiwi fruits, revered in traditional Chinese medicine for their healing effect on stomach and breast cancer.
**10 g carbs per 100 g**

**Melons** are an excellent low-carb and highly nutritious fruit. Most melons are natural diuretics, so they are powerful cleansers and detoxifiers. Because of their high water content, they are also great for rehydration and hardly need any diluting when used in juices or smoothies. Orange melons such as Galia are high in betacarotene. Watermelons have anticoagulant properties and all melons are antiviral and antibacterial.
**5–7 g carbs per 100 g**

**Papaya** aids digestion as it contains the enzyme papain; this helps to break down protein. Papaya is thought to help protect against cancer and replenishes lost levels of vitamin C.
**8 g carbs per 100 g**

**Pineapples** can be a little high in carbohydrates but the health benefits and their fantastic flavor justify including moderate amounts of pineapple in many juices and smoothies. They are antiinflammatory, antiviral, and antibacterial and known for being able to help dissolve blood clots. They contain the digestive enzyme bromelain, which is essential in the digestion of protein.
**10 g carbs per 100 g**

**Tomatoes** are very versatile foods and mix well with most other fruits and vegetables in juices. They are thought to lower the risk of cancer and heart disease due to the presence of lycopene, which fights off free radicals.
**3.5 g carbs per 100 g**

# Top 10 low-carb vegetables

**Bean and seed sprouts** contain high levels of nutrients that are easy for the body to absorb. They are superfoods with a high protein, enzyme, vitamin, and mineral content. They are thought to protect against cancer and support every system in the body. Their contribution to maintaining a healthy immune system can be huge and sprouts should be included in every low-carb meal plan.
**0.4 g carbs per 100 g**

**Beets** are high in folate. They have a regulating effect on the digestive system and stimulate and strengthen the bowel, moving toxins out of the system. Kidney and liver function can be improved and the blood cleaned and fortified by regular consumption of beets. Another benefit is that beets aid fat metabolism. It may not be the lowest carb ingredient in the book, but even adding a little beet can help increase the nutritional value of any juice.
**7.5 g carbs per 100 g**

**Bell peppers** are rich in vitamin C and have antioxidant properties. They help guard against macular degeneration and respiratory infections. They also help to keep arteries uncongested and are said to be effective in helping conditions such as asthma, bronchitis, and even the common cold. Bell peppers are rich in natural silicones, which help to keep nails, skin, and hair glossy and healthy.
**6.5 g carbs per 100 g**

**Broccoli** is a member of the cruciferous family of vegetables, which are full of antioxidants, and it is high in vitamin C. It is sensible to have a regular intake of this vegetable if you want to guard against lung, breast, and colon cancer. It has been reported that it can even deactivate cancer cells. On a low-carb regime, broccoli is useful as it helps to regulate insulin and blood sugar. A superb superfood.
**1.8 g carbs per 100 g**

**Cabbage** has a high reputation as a cancer fighter. It can regulate estrogen metabolism and discourage the formation of polyps. Cabbage is best eaten raw and ideally should be included in the diet 2–3 times per week. As a detoxifier it is massively effective, and it is an excellent ingredient in juices. The downside? The taste, but if you mix it with more pleasant tasting fruits and vegetables, the juice can be very palatable.
**4 g carbs per 100 g**

**Carrots** rate very highly on the carb scale when cooked, but less so when raw, and are too good a juicing ingredient to ignore. Used carefully and moderately, carrots are nutritional power houses. Their antioxidant capabilities stem from a very high betacarotene content. They may help fight cancer, protect arteries, battle infections, and boost immunity. They are said to eliminate some bacteria in the colon and facilitate elimination of intestinal parasites. Carrots blend well with virtually all other ingredients so are excellent ingredients for juicing.
**6 g carbs per 100 g**

**Celeriac, celery, and fennel** are all excellent for cleansing the digestive system of uric acid and are fabulous low-carb ingredients. All three have a high potassium content and so are good for lowering high blood pressure. If you retain excess fluid and suffer from regular bloating their diuretic effect is powerful; if you wish to detoxify your body, they should form the basis of your juices.
**Celeriac 2.3 g carbs per 100 g; celery 0.9 g per 100 g; fennel 1.8 g per 100 g**

**Cucumber** provides a versatile low-carb base for many refreshing juices and smoothies. It is naturally diuretic, will stimulate elimination of toxins via the urinary tract, and contains compounds essential for healthy hair and skin nutrition.
**1.5 g carbs per 100 g**

**Leafy green vegetables** should be an integral part of your daily diet. Spinach, kale, collard greens, and bok choy are all rich in antioxidants, full of lutein and betacarotene, and may help battle cancer and regulate estrogen. Even if you prefer sweeter fruit-based juices, try to have a couple of green juices each week. Your system will thank you for it.
**1.6 g carbs per 100 g**

**Lettuce** comes in all shapes and sizes and contains high levels of vitamin C, betacarotene, flavonols, and folic acid. Vary the lettuces you juice as they all contain slightly different phytonutrients. Essentially all have antioxidant properties, cleanse the digestive tract, and enhance the activity of bacteria in the gut.
**1.7 g carbs per 100 g**

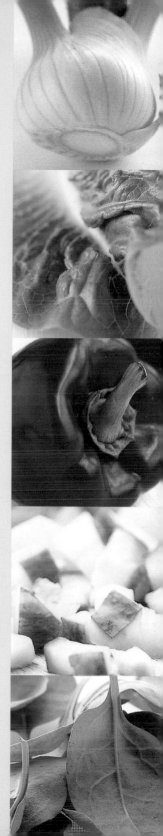

# Top 10 low-carb ingredients

**Coconut** has tremendous antiviral properties due to its high content of lauric acid, which fights viral pathogens. Coconut milk and powder can add exotic flavor and richness to your smoothies, but remember that they are high in saturated fats (although they are the healthiest saturated fats you could choose and have been shown to have a positive effect on health in general).
**Coconut milk 4.9 g carbs per 100 g**

**Garlic** has been called the "wonder drug," and it is one of the world's oldest medicines. Raw garlic is a powerful antibiotic that fights bacteria, parasites, and viruses. Two or three garlic cloves a day lessen the chance of heart attacks and strokes, and contain many anticancer compounds including allyl sulphides. Garlic boosts immunity, lowers cholesterol and blood pressure. It is at its most powerful raw, although it is still very potent when cooked. Add a raw garlic clove or two to savory juices for a real health kick.
**Negligible carbs**

**Ginger** has long been used by Asians for chest congestion, colds, diarrhea, and nausea. It is antiinflammatory and naturally antibiotic, and boosts HDL—good cholesterol. Reputedly an antidepressant, it strengthens the immune system and can add anything from gentle warmth to fiery heat to savory juices or smoothies, depending on how much is used.
**Negligible carbs**

**Herbs, spices, and essences** are fabulous ways to add flavor to juices and smoothies. Normally they contain only small amounts of nutrients because they are used in such minute quantities, but some stimulate the appetite, encourage the flow of digestive juices, and are reputed to have healing properties. Fresh herbs such as mint, basil, and parsley can individualize low-carb drinks, as can spices and essences such as vanilla and almond.
**Negligible carbs**

**Low-carb ice creams**—look out for these in your local supermarket or health-food stores. They can be blended with fruit for extra creamy low-carb smoothies.
**About 1 g carbs per 100 g**

**Nuts** are a concentrated food source. They are full of protein, vitamins, unsaturated omega-3 fatty acids, and minerals (especially selenium, an effective antioxidant). They reduce levels of bad cholesterol, and contain anticancer and heart-protecting qualities. Add freshly ground nuts to smoothies for flavor and nutrition.
**Cashews 18 g carbs per 100 g; almonds 7 g per 100 g**

**Seeds** can be added to most smoothies for super boosts of many vital nutrients. Sesame, pumpkin, sunflower, and flax seeds are rich in protein, A, D, E, and B complex vitamins, minerals, and unsaturated omega-3 fatty acids. They should be kept in the refrigerator or they will oxidize, spoiling their taste and nutritional value.
**Sesame 0.9 g carbs per 100 g; sunflower 18 g per 100 g; pumpkin 15 g per 100 g**

**Soy products** contain vitamins and minerals in natural relationship similar to the human body's needs. They are high in isoflavones which mimic the action of the female sex hormone, estrogen (good for menopausal women), reduce insulin levels, decrease arteriosclerosis, and lower levels of LDL—bad cholesterol. Soy can help lower the risk of cancer, relieve constipation, regulate blood sugar, and is a major source of protein for vegetarians. Try soy milk, yogurt, ice cream, and tofu in fruit-based smoothies for a low-carb but high-protein boost.
**Soy milk 9 g carbs per 100 g; tofu 0.7g per 100 g; soy yogurt 3.5 g per 100 g**

**Whey protein powder** contains high value biological protein which encourages the formation of lean muscle mass. It increases glutathione levels which give added support to the immune system and helps to build healthy collagen. Whey protein powder is available from health-food stores and comes in a variety of flavors. Add to smoothies for a protein kick.
**About 9 g carbs per 100 g**

**Yogurt** disables and kills unwanted bacteria and makes an excellent base for many smoothies. The probiotics in live yogurt may help to inhibit the formation of cancer-causing compounds; they also help to detoxify the body by reducing inflammation and encouraging the elimination of intestinal parasites. Yogurt stimulates the kidneys, thus aiding digestion. Avoid sweetened yogurts as the sugar is antagonistic to the B vitamins made from the bacteria naturally found in yogurt.
**Natural live yogurt 7.5 g carbs per 100 g**

# Smoothies

# Cucumber, lemon, & mint smoothie

**1½ cucumbers**
(about 8 oz), peeled

**½ lemon**

**3–4 fresh mint leaves,**
plus more to decorate

**2–3 ice cubes**

**Makes 1¼ cups**

Dice the cucumber roughly, and squeeze the lemon. Put them in a blender with the mint leaves and ice cubes and whiz to a super cool smoothie. Decorate with more mint leaves if you desire.

This light refreshing drink is great for kidney health as it stimulates elimination of toxins—this is vital if you are following a high-protein regime.

**Nutritional Values**

Carbs 4.25 g  •  Kcals 27  •  Magnesium 22 mg  •  Vitamin C 16 mg  •  Calcium 47 mg

**star low carb**

# Tiger smoothie

1 medium **papaya**

1 **passion fruit**

½ **lime**

2–3 **ice cubes**

Makes ¾ cup

Cut the papaya in half, scoop out and discard the seeds and skin. Chop the flesh roughly and put it into a blender. Cut the passion fruit in half and spoon the juice and seeds into the blender. Squeeze in the lime and add the ice cubes. Whiz until smooth then pour into a glass.

Papaya is full of enzymes and has valuable antiparasitic qualities, while the lime juice and passion fruit ensure this smoothie is full of flavor.

**Nutritional Values**

Carbs 15 g ● Kcals 65 ● Magnesium 25 mg ● Vitamin C 105 mg

# Raspberry shake

1 cup **raspberries**

⅔ cup **soy milk**

Makes ¾ **cup**

**Freeze the raspberries, then put them into a blender, reserving 2 or 3 for decoration. Pour in the soy milk and whiz together. Tip into a tumbler and decorate with the remaining raspberries.**

Raspberries help to relieve menstrual cramps and soy beans are full of phytoestrogens that may help prevent breast and ovarian cancers. Both are very good for female health.

**Nutritional Values**

Carbs 6 g ● Kcals 87 ● Vitamin C 22 mg ● Calcium 47 mg ● Potassium 180 mg

# Grapefruit & cucumber crush

1 ⅓ **cucumbers** (about 7 oz), peeled

½ cup **grapefruit juice**

6 **ice cubes**

Makes ¾ **cup**

**Chop the cucumber roughly and put it into a blender. Pour in the grapefruit juice and add the ice cubes. Whiz until the ice is coarsely crushed then tip into a tumbler.**

This is a great summertime drink that cleanses and refreshes the system. Served over ice it is a perfect accompaniment to a low-carb snack such as nuts.

**Nutritional Values**

Carbs 5 g ● Kcals 26.5 ● Calcium 25 mg ● Vitamin C 17.5 mg

**star low carb**

# Cranberry smoothie

½ cup **cranberries**

3 tablespoons **plain strained yogurt**

½ cup **soy milk**

3 **ice cubes**

**artificial sweetener,** to taste

**Put the cranberries into a blender. Add the yogurt, soy milk, and ice cubes and whiz together. Taste, then add artificial sweetener if required and whiz again. Pour into a tall tumbler and serve immediately.**

Makes 1¼ cups

This delicious smoothie is excellent for the kidneys and high in bone-boosting calcium.

**Nutritional Values**

Carbs 7 g • Kcals 100 • Vitamin C 13 mg • Calcium 100 mg

# Beet & berry smoothie

1 small **beet** (about 2 oz)

¾ cup **blueberries**

1 cup **raspberries**

2–3 **ice cubes**

**blueberries,** to decorate

**Makes 1 cup**

**Juice the beet then pour it into a blender. Add the blueberries, raspberries, and ice cubes to the blender and whiz together. Pour into a glass and decorate with blueberries, if using.**

This deep red juice is a real blood booster. Beet builds up red blood cells and the berries contain natural aspirin, working against clots and strokes.

**Nutritional Values**

Carbs 15 g  ●  Kcals 75  ●  Vitamin C 51 mg  ●  Calcium 47mg

# Apple & avocado smoothie

½ cup **apple juice**

1 small **avocado**

2 **ice cubes**

apple slice,
to decorate

**Makes ¾ cup**

Pour the apple juice into a blender. Cut the avocado in half, remove the pit, and spoon in the flesh. Add the ice cubes and whiz together. Pour into a glass and decorate with an apple slice.

This smoothie makes a fantastic meal replacement. For added protein, add a raw organic egg to the blend.

**Nutritional Values**

Carbs 11 g ● Kcals 228 ● Vitamin C 20 mg ● Calcium 18 mg

# Blueberry & mint smoothie

¾ cup **blueberries**

⅔ cup **soy milk**

small bunch of **mint**

Makes 1 cup

Freeze the blueberries, then tip them into a blender and pour in the soy milk. Pull the mint leaves off their stalks, reserving one or two sprigs for decoration, and add to the blender. Whiz together, then serve in a tall glass, decorated with the reserved mint sprigs.

The addition of mint to this delightful low-carb smoothie makes it a most refreshing drink.

**Nutritional Values**

Carbs 8.5 g  ●  Kcals 78  ●  Vitamin C 17 mg  ●  Calcium 2.5 mg

# Coconut & pineapple smoothie

4 oz **pineapple**, peeled and cored

½ cup **coconut milk**

½ cup **soy milk**

½ teaspoon **toasted coconut**, to decorate

**Makes 1¼ cups**

**Chop the pineapple into chunks and freeze. Put the frozen chunks into a blender. Add the coconut milk and soy milk and whiz together. Pour into a large glass and sprinkle with toasted coconut.**

If you like pina coladas, you'll love this tasty smoothie. You could also add a few drops of rum flavoring for extra authenticity.

**Nutritional Values**

Carbs 15 g   ●   Kcals 95   ●   Vitamin C 14 mg   ●   Calcium 60 mg

# Mango lassi

| 1 small **mango** | Cut a slice either side of the mango seed and score the flesh into cubes. Bend the skin back to separate the cubes then spoon them into a blender. Pour in the yogurt and iced water. Add the rosewater and ground cardamon, if using, and whiz together. Transfer to a large glass. |

1 small **mango**

⅓ cup **live plain yogurt**

⅓ cup **iced still water**

1 tablespoon **rosewater** (optional)

¼ teaspoon **ground cardamom** (optional)

**Makes about 1 cup**

Cut a slice either side of the mango seed and score the flesh into cubes. Bend the skin back to separate the cubes then spoon them into a blender. Pour in the yogurt and iced water. Add the rosewater and ground cardamon, if using, and whiz together. Transfer to a large glass.

Lassi is a traditional Indian beverage that is served chilled. A splash of rosewater and a dusting of ground cardamom add an extra taste sensation to this mango version.

**Nutritional Values**

Carbs 14.5 g ● Kcals 81 ● Vitamin C 23 mg ● Calcium 168 mg

# Cucumber lassi

1 **cucumber** (about 5 oz), peeled

½ cup **live plain yogurt**

½ cup **iced still water**

handful of **mint leaves**

½ teaspoon **ground cumin**

squeeze of **fresh lemon juice**

**Makes 2 x ¾ cup**

Chop the cucumber roughly and put it into a blender. Add the yogurt and iced water. Pull the mint leaves off their stalks and reserve a few for decoration, if liked. Chop the remainder roughly and put them into the blender. Add the cumin and lemon juice and whiz together. Pour into 2 tall glasses.

This smoothie is the perfect accompaniment to a spicy Indian meal as it cools the palate—or you can just enjoy it on its own as a satisfying summertime drink.

**Nutritional Values (per serving)**

Carbs 7.5 g ● Kcals 50 ● Magnesium 20 mg ● Calcium 156 mg

# Nut & berry smoothie

⅔ cup **strawberries**

2 tablespoons **smooth peanut butter**

¼ cup **whey protein powder**

⅔ cup **still water**

2–3 **ice cubes**

half a **strawberry**, to decorate

**Makes 1¼ cups**

Roughly chop the strawberries and put them into a blender. Spoon in the peanut butter and whey protein powder. Pour in the water and add the ice cubes. Whiz all the ingredients together and serve in a small glass, decorated with half a strawberry, if you desire.

If you want a quick breakfast replacement, this is the perfect smoothie as it is full of protein and will easily keep you going until lunchtime.

**Nutritional Values**

Carbs 12 g ● Kcals 282 ● Vitamin C 77 mg ● Calcium 125 mg

# Peach & tofu smoothie

1 **peach**, skinned and pitted

½ cup **tofu**

¼ cup **low-carb vanilla ice cream**

½ cup **still water**

few drops of **natural almond extract**

Makes 1¼ **cups**

**Roughly chop the peach flesh and put it in a blender with the tofu and the ice cream. Pour in the water and add a little almond extract then whiz together. Transfer to 2 glasses. Serve over ice if desired.**

Full of enzymes and protein, this smoothie has the taste of summer and is made extra creamy by the addition of home-made ice cream.

**Nutritional Values**

Carbs 8.7 g  ●  Kcals 230  ●  Vitamin C 32 mg  ●  Calcium 76 mg

# Rhubarb smoothie

½ cup **stewed rhubarb**

⅓ cup **live plain yogurt**

2 drops of **vanilla extract**

**artificial sweetener,** to taste

2–3 **ice cubes**

Makes ¾ **cup**

Put the stewed rhubarb into a blender with the yogurt and add a few drops of vanilla extract and a little artificial sweetener to taste. Whiz together with a couple of ice cubes then pour into a tall glass.

Rhubarb must be cooked as it is full of oxalic acid when raw. Combined with yogurt it makes a delicious smoothie that is full of useful bacteria for intestinal health.

**Nutritional Values**

Carbs 6.7 g  ●  Kcals 48  ●  Magnesium 20 mg  ●  Calcium 165 g

# Melon & almond smoothie

4 oz **Galia melon**, skinned and deseeded

½ cup **almond milk**

**melon slice**, to decorate

**Makes 1 cup**

**Chop the melon into chunks and freeze. Put the frozen melon chunks into a blender with the almond milk and whiz together. Pour into a tall glass. Serve immediately, decorated with a melon slice.**

This calming and refreshing smoothie is perfect at the end of a hard day or after strenuous exercise.

**Nutritional Values**

Carbs 5.6 g ● Kcals 24 ● Vitamin C 15 mg ● Calcium 13 mg

**star low carb**

# Mandarin & litchi frappé

½ cup **mandarin oranges**, canned in natural juice

¼ cup **litchis**, canned in natural juice

2 **ice cubes**

**Makes ⅔ cup**

**Put the mandarin oranges and the litchis with their canning juices into a blender with the ice cubes and whiz together. Pour into a glass and serve.**

Always make sure that fruit is canned in water or in its own juice; sugar-laden syrup is full of carbs.

**Nutritional Values**

Carbs 14 g  ●  Kcals 61  ●  Vitamin C 42 mg  ●  Calcium 20 mg

# Choco-cherry shake

½ cup **cherries**, pitted

½ cup **soy milk**

¼ cup **chocolate-flavored whey protein powder**

2–3 **ice cubes**

**cocoa powder,** to decorate

Makes 1 cup

**Put the cherries into a blender. Pour in the soy milk, add the whey protein powder and the ice cubes and whiz together. Pour into a glass and sprinkle with a little cocoa powder.**

If you are a shake-and-burger fan, this is the smoothie for you. Just don't have the bun.

**Nutritional Values**

Carbs 15 g ● Kcals 173 ● Vitamin C 11 mg ● Calcium 65 mg

# Apricot & almond smoothie

2–3 **apricots** (about 4 oz), skinned and pitted

¼ cup **ground almonds**

3 tablespoons **soy milk**

3 tablespoons **soy yogurt**

2 **ice cubes**

**chopped almonds,** to decorate

Makes ¾ **cup**

**Roughly chop the apricot flesh. Put it into a blender with the ground almonds, soy milk, and soy yogurt. Whiz together with the ice cubes and pour into a tall glass. Decorate with the chopped almonds and serve immediately.**

This smoothie is highly nutritious—apricots are full of betacarotene and almonds are a concentrated source of protein, unsaturated fats, and minerals.

**Nutritional Values**

Carbs 11 g ● Kcals 250 ● Protein 10 g ● Magnesium 94 mg ● Calcium 88 mg

# Virgin Mary

¼ **red bell pepper**, cored and deseeded

½ **cucumber**, peeled

5 **scallions**

½ cup **tomato juice**

splash of **lemon juice**

splash of **hot pepper sauce**

splash of **Worcestershire sauce**

**salt and pepper**

Roughly chop the bell pepper and the cucumber. Roughly chop the scallions, reserving a few shreds for a garnish. Pour the tomato juice, the red pepper, cucumber, and scallions into a blender and whiz. Taste, then season with lemon juice, hot pepper sauce, Worcestershire sauce, and salt and pepper according to your taste. Garnish with the remaining scallion.

Makes ¾ cup

This is a great drink to serve with a high-protein brunch or as an aperitif with a few olives and some nuts.

**Nutritional Values**

Carbs 7 g ● Kcals 40 ● Vitamin C 86 mg ● Calcium 35 mg

# Guacamole smoothie

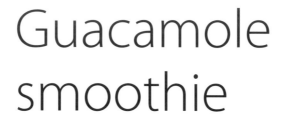

5 **scalllions**

½ small **chili pepper**

½ medium **avocado**

½ cup **tomato juice**

a few **cilantro leaves,** plus extra to decorate

2 **ice cubes**

Makes ¾ cup

Roughly chop the scallions. Place in a blender with the chili pepper and add the avocado flesh and the tomato juice. Add the cilantro leaves and ice cubes and whiz together. Pour into a glass and decorate with chopped cilantro.

This Mexican-inspired savory smoothie is full of nutrients and very low in carbs. The combination of tomato and avocado ensures a good boost of antioxidants.

**Nutritional Values**

Carbs 5.8 g ● Kcals 167 ● Vitamin C 46 mg ● Calcium 36 mg

**star low carb**

# Watermelon cooler

4 oz **watermelon**, skinned and deseeded

²/₃ cup **strawberries**, hulled

½ cup **still water**

small handful of **mint** or **tarragon leaves**

Makes 1¼ cups

Chop the watermelon into chunks and roughly chop the strawberries. Freeze the melon and strawberries until solid. Place the frozen melon and strawberries in a blender with the water, add the mint or tarragon and whiz until smooth. Pour into two tumblers, decorate and serve immediately.

This drink can be served as a smoothie or you can make it into an iced snack. The addition of mint leaves works well, or you could try tarragon to give the smoothie an unusual twist.

**Nutritional Values**

Carbs 14 g  •  Kcals 64  •  Vitamin C 56 mg  •  Calcium 26 mg

# Vanilla & litchi froth

¼ cup **litchis**, canned in water or their own juice

¼ cup **vanilla-flavored whey protein powder**

½ cup **sparkling mineral water**

2–3 **ice cubes**

**Makes ¾ cup**

**Put the litchis with the canned juice into a blender, add the whey protein powder, mineral water, and ice cubes and whiz together. Pour into a tall glass and serve immediately.**

The litchis add a delicate sweetness to this protein shake, while the sparkling water gives it lightness.

**Nutritional Values**

Carbs 9 g ● Kcals 120 ● Calcium 103 mg ● Magnesium 104 mg ● Vitamin C 22 mg

# Juices

# Melon berry cherry juice

4 oz **watermelon,** skinned and deseeded

¼ cup **cherries,** pitted

⅓ cup **blackberries,** hulled

**ice cubes,** to serve

**watermelon slice,** to garnish

**Makes ⅔ cup**

**Roughly chop the flesh of the watermelon. Juice the fruits, then serve in a glass over ice, garnished with a slice of watermelon.**

Drink a glass of this rich juice instead of wine. The melon is very good for cleansing the system while the cherries have a whole host of benefits, especially if you suffer from gout.

**Nutritional Values**

Carbs 15 g  ●  Kcals 67  ●  Calcium 34 mg  ●  Vitamin C 21 mg

# Celery, ginger, & pineapple juice

5 **celery stalks**, trimmed

4 oz **pineapple**, peeled and cored

1 inch piece of **fresh ginger root**, peeled

**crushed ice**

**Makes ¾ cup**

**Cut the celery into lengths and the pineapple into chunks. Chop the ginger roughly. Juice all the ingredients then whiz in a blender with a little crushed ice.**

This drink is a brilliant digestive as the pineapple contains bromelain, an enzyme which is very similar to stomach acid and helps to break down protein.

**Nutritional Values**

Carbs 14 g ● Kcals 64 ● Calcium 75 mg ● Vitamin C 25 mg

# Summer strawberry juice

⅔ cup **strawberries**, hulled

2 **tomatoes** (about 7 oz)

a few **basil leaves**

**ice cubes,** to serve

**Makes ¾ cup**

**Juice the strawberries with the tomatoes and a few basil leaves, reserving 1 basil leaf for decoration. Serve in a tumbler over ice and decorate with the reserved basil leaf.**

This colorful juice is full of phytonutrients, including lycopene which has been proven to contain anti-cancer properties.

**Nutritional Values**

Carbs 12g ● Kcals 61 ● Vitamin C 111 mg ● Calcium 30 mg ● Magnesium 24 mg

# Pineapple, lettuce, & celery juice

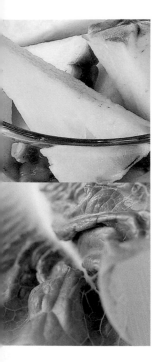

4 oz **pineapple**, peeled and cored

4 oz **lettuce**

5 **celery stalks**, trimmed

**ice cubes**, to serve

**celery stalk**, to garnish

**Makes ¾ cup**

**Chop the pineapple roughly. Separate the lettuce into leaves. Cut the celery into lengths. Juice all the ingredients and serve in a tall glass over ice.**

This juice is both cleansing and detoxifying: it is also calming as lettuce is one of nature's natural tranquilizers.

**Nutritional Values**

Carbs 15 g  ●  Kcals 77  ●  Vitamin C 32 mg  ●  Calcium 108 mg

# Orange, celeriac, & bean sprout juice

1 small **orange**, peeled

4 oz **celeriac**, peeled

2 cups **alfalfa sprouts**

**extra orange slice,** to decorate

Makes ¾ cup

**Separate the orange into segments. Cut the celeriac into chunks. Rinse the alfalfa sprouts. Juice all the ingredients, pour the juice into a glass, and decorate with an extra orange slice. Drink immediately to reap the full nutritional benefits.**

Combining orange with celeriac and alfalfa sprouts gives you a low-carb juice with a great taste that is also packed with healthy enzymes.

**Nutritional Values**

Carbs 11 g ● Kcals 79 ● Vitamin C 70 mg ● Calcium 120 mg

# Citrus–veg juice

¼ **grapefruit**, peeled

4 oz **lettuce**

3 **celery stalks**, trimmed

½ **pear**

2–3 **ice cubes**

Makes ¾ cup

Segment the grapefruit. Separate the lettuce into leaves. Cut the celery into lengths. Quarter the pear. Juice all the ingredients and pour into a glass. Serve over ice.

Pears are quite high in carbs, but in this recipe they are used for a hint of natural sweetness, and grapefruit, celery, and lettuce are very low in carbs.

**Nutritional Values**

Carbs 14.5 g ● Kcals 71 ● Vitamin C 42 mg ● Calcium 88 mg

# Cranberry, apple, & lettuce juice

½ **apple**

4 oz **lettuce**

¼ cup **cranberries**

2 **ice cubes**

Makes ¾ **cup**

**Cut the apple into slices. Separate the lettuce into leaves. Juice the apple, lettuce, and cranberries, then pour the juice into a blender, add the ice and whiz together. Serve immediately.**

Apples are an excellent base for juices as they blend well with almost all other ingredients. They are also good for cleansing the digestive tract.

**Nutritional Values**

Carbs 11 g ● Kcals 61 ● Vitamin C 18 mg ● Calcium 64 mg

# Pineapple & lettuce juice

3 oz **pineapple**, peeled and cored

7 oz **lettuce**

2–3 **ice cubes**

**mint leaves,** to decorate

Makes ¾ cup

Chop the pineapple into chunks and separate the lettuce into leaves. Juice the pineapple and lettuce, pour into a glass, and serve over ice. Decorate with mint leaves. Alternatively, put the pineapple and lettuce into a blender with 2–3 ice cubes and a few mint leaves and whiz to make a refreshing smoothie.

Pineapple should always be combined with a more neutral ingredient such as lettuce, as it is high in acids that can damage tooth enamel if taken in excess.

**Nutritional Values**

Carbs 10 g  ●  Kcals 58  ●  Vitamin C 19 mg  ●  Calcium 69 mg

# Raspberry & celeriac juice

1¼ cups **raspberries**

5 oz **celeriac**, peeled

2–3 **ice cubes**

Makes 1 cup

Freeze the raspberries. Cut the celeriac into chunks and juice. Pour the juice into a blender and whiz with the raspberries and a little ice. Pour into a glass and serve immediately.

This juice is sharp and refreshing. Try it if you have a headache, as it is full of antiinflammatory compounds and works as a natural aspirin.

**Nutritional Values**

Carbs 10 g ● Kcals 64 ● Vitamin C 69 mg ● Calcium 97 mg

# Kiwi fruit & lettuce juice

1 **kiwi fruit**, peeled

7 oz **lettuce**

2–3 **ice cubes**

**kiwi slice,** to decorate

**Makes ¾ cup**

Roughly chop the flesh of the kiwi fruit. Separate the lettuce into leaves. Juice both ingredients and pour into a glass over ice. Decorate with a kiwi slice and serve immediately.

Kiwi fruit are rich in vitamin C. Vitamin C is very important for anyone on a high-protein diet as this means the body needs extra vitamin C to function effectively.

**Nutritional Values**

Carbs 14 g ● Kcals 77 ● Vitamin C 69 mg ● Calcium 81 mg

# Pineapple & alfalfa juice

5 oz **pineapple**, peeled and cored

2½ cups **alfalfa sprouts**

2 **ice cubes**

3 tablespoons **still water**

**Makes 1 cup**

**Cut the pineapple into chunks and juice it. Put the juice in a blender, add the alfalfa sprouts, ice cubes, and water and whiz together. Pour into a glass and serve.**

Pineapples are antiinflammatory, antiviral, and antibacterial, making them a superb addition to a healthy diet.

**Nutritional Values**

Carbs 15 g ● Kcals 97 ● Vitamin C 21 mg ● Calcium 76 mg

# Orange & passion fruit sparkler

1 small **orange**, peeled

½ **passion fruit**

½ cup **sparkling mineral water**

2–3 **ice cubes**

Makes ¾ cup

Segment and juice the orange. Scoop the flesh out of the passion fruit and press the pulp through a strainer to extract the juice. Pour the orange juice into a jug and mix with the passion fruit juice and sparkling water. Pour into a glass over ice.

As well as being a great source of vitamin C, carotenoids, and bioflavanoids, all of which help fight cancer, oranges also lower blood cholesterol.

**Nutritional Values**

Carbs 11.5 g ● Kcals 55 ● Vitamin C 65 mg ● Calcium 52 mg

# Blackberry, apple, & celeriac juice

²⁄₃ cup **blackberries**

4 oz **celeriac**, peeled

½ **apple**

2 **ice cubes**

**extra frozen blackberries,**
to decorate

**Makes ¾ cup**

Freeze the blackberries. Cut the celeriac into chunks. Cut the apple into pieces then juice with the celeriac. Put the juice into a blender with the frozen blackberries and a couple of ice cubes and whiz together. Pour into a glass and decorate with extra blackberries.

This juice will remind you of old-fashioned blackberry and apple pie, but without the high-carb pastry and sugar.

**Nutritional Values**

Carbs 13 g  ●  Kcals 66  ●  Vitamin C 32 mg  ●  Calcium 83 mg

# Pear, celery, & ginger juice

1 small **pear**

2 **celery stalks**, trimmed

1 inch piece of **fresh ginger root**, peeled

**ice cubes**

Makes ¾ **cup**

Cut the celery into lengths. Chop the ginger roughly. Juice together the pear, celery, and ginger. Pour into a glass over ice. Alternatively, whiz the juice in a blender with 2–3 ice cubes.

Pears are a gentle, natural laxative; celery is a diuretic, while ginger promotes good digestion, making this a great juice for keeping your system balanced and regular.

**Nutritional Values**

Carbs 11 g  ●  Kcals 50  ●  Vitamin C 18 mg  ●  Calcium 72 mg

# Cherry & cranberry fizz

⅓ cup **cherries**, pitted

⅓ cup **cranberries**

½ cup **sparkling mineral water**

2–3 **ice cubes**

Makes ¾ **cup**

**Juice the cherries and the cranberries. Pour the juice into a jug, add the sparkling water, and mix together. Serve in a glass over ice.**

This juice is fabulous for anyone who likes a sour-tasting drink, and it has the added benefit of keeping the urinary tract free from infection.

**Nutritional Values**

Carbs 11 g ● Kcals 47 ● Vitamin C 18 mg ● Calcium 19 mg

# Broccoli, parsnip, & apple juice

½ **parsnip**, peeled

½ **apple**

5 oz **broccoli**, trimmed

2 **ice cubes**

Makes ¾ cup

Cut the parsnip into chunks and the apple into quarters. Juice together the broccoli, parsnip, and apple then transfer the juice to a blender and whiz with the ice cubes to make a creamy juice.

This rich sweet juice is bursting with vitamin C and broccoli naturally regulates insulin and blood sugar.

**Nutritional Values**

Carbs 14 g ● Kcals 104 ● Vitamin C 141 mg ● Calcium 106 mg

# Tomato, carrot, & red pepper juice

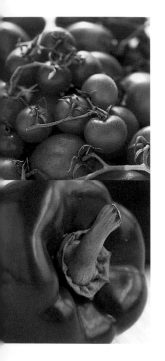

½ **red bell pepper**, cored and deseeded

1 small **carrot**

1 **tomato**

2–3 **ice cubes**

**carrot ribbon,** to decorate

**Makes ¾ cup**

**Chop the pepper roughly. Cut the carrot into chunks. Juice together the red pepper, carrot, and tomato. Pour into a glass over ice, decorate with a carrot ribbon, and serve immediately.**

This delicious drink is full of antioxidants. Add some onion, garlic, and ice and blend and you have a tasty gazpacho-style smoothie.

**Nutritional Values**

Carbs 13.5 g ● Kcals 66 ● Vitamin C 160 mg ● Calcium 27 mg

# Celery, fennel, & pineapple juice

4 **celery stalks**, trimmed

4 oz **fennel**

3 oz **pineapple**, peeled and cored

2–3 **ice cubes**

Makes ¾ **cup**

**Cut the celery into lengths. Cut the fennel into chunks. Juice the celery, fennel, and pineapple and pour into a glass over ice. Serve immediately.**

Both celery and fennel are very effective diuretics. Fennel also has appetite-controlling properties that may help if you are trying to lose weight.

**Nutritional Values**

Carbs 5 g ● Kcals 49 ● Vitamin C 24 mg ● Calcium 67 mg

star low-carb

# Celery & celeriac leafy juice

4 **celery stalks**, trimmed

5 oz **celeriac**, peeled

4 oz **lettuce**

4 oz **spinach**

2–3 **ice cubes**

**Makes 1 cup**

Cut the celery into lengths and the celeriac into chunks. Separate the lettuce into leaves. Juice together the celery, celeriac, lettuce, and spinach. Transfer the juice to a blender and whiz with the ice cubes.

This bright green juice is good as a weekly detoxifying tonic. Like most green vegetable juices, blending it with ice will make it more creamy and palatable.

**Nutritional Values**

Carbs 7.5 g ● Kcals 73 ● Vitamin C 60 mg ● Calcium 300 mg

# Cabbage, apple, & cinnamon juice

8 oz **green cabbage**

½ **apple**

2 **ice cubes**

**ground cinnamon,** plus extra to decorate

Makes ¾ **cup**

**Separate the cabbage into leaves and cut the apple into pieces. Juice together then pour the juice into a blender and whiz with the ice cubes and a sprinkling of cinnamon. Serve decorated with a sprinkling of cinnamon.**

This tasty combination of flavors is a good way to enjoy cabbage juice. Cabbage is a superfood which is thought to fight cancer, and particularly cancer of the colon.

**Nutritional Values**

Carbs 13.5 g ● Kcals 76 ● Vitamin C 126 mg ● Calcium 108 mg

# Cucumber & kiwi fruit juice

**1½ cucumbers**
(about 7 oz), peeled

**1 kiwi fruit**, peeled

**2–3 ice cubes**

Makes ¾ cup

Cut the cucumber into chunks. Juice the cucumber and kiwi fruit and serve over ice. Alternatively, pour the juice into a blender and whiz with the ice to make a smoothie.

Served over ice with lemon, this juice has a refreshing clean taste and will revive you when you are feeling sluggish and dehydrated.

## Nutritional Values

Carbs 13 g ● Kcals 69 ● Vitamin C 63 mg ● Calcium 61 mg

# Carrot, celeriac, & celery juice

1 **carrot**

4 oz **celeriac**, peeled

4 **celery stalks**, trimmed

2–3 **ice cubes**

**celery stalk,** to decorate

Makes ¾ **cup**

Cut the carrot and celeriac into chunks. Cut the celery into lengths. Juice together the carrot, celeriac, and celery and serve over ice decorated with a short celery stalk.

This classic, low-carb vegetable combination gives you the taste of carrot juice but without the higher carb count.

**Nutritional Values**

Carbs 9 g ● Kcals 55 ● Vitamin C 26 mg ● Calcium 115 mg

# Carrot & lettuce juice

1 **carrot**

8 oz **lettuce**

2–3 **ice cubes**

**chopped cilantro leaves,** to decorate

Cut the carrot into chunks and separate the lettuce into leaves. Juice together and serve over ice decorated with a little chopped cilantro.

**Makes ¾ cup**

Carrots are forbidden on many low-carb diets because of their high GI value, but if you combine them with low-carb lettuce, you can benefit from their high nutrient content.

**Nutritional Values**

Carbs 11 g  ●  Kcals 63  ●  Vitamin C 16 mg  ●  Calcium 81 mg

# Tomato & celery juice

8 **celery stalks**, trimmed

2 **tomatoes**

**celery salt** and **black pepper**

**Tabasco sauce,** to taste

**ice cubes** (optional)

**Makes ¾ cup**

Cut the celery into lengths. Juice the celery with the tomato and season with celery salt, black pepper, and Tabasco sauce. Serve over ice or at room temperature.

Tomatoes and celery are both great low-carb ingredients and this juice is fantastic as an accompaniment to a healthy salad, or as a predinner appetizer.

**Nutritional Values**

Carbs 8 g  ●  Kcals 48  ●  Vitamin C 50 mg  ●  Calcium 96 mg

# Broccoli, lettuce, & celery juice

4 oz **lettuce**

4 **celery stalks**, trimmed

5 oz **broccoli**, trimmed

2–3 **ice cubes**

**Makes 1 cup**

Separate the lettuce into leaves. Cut the celery into lengths. Juice together the broccoli, lettuce, and celery. Serve the juice over ice or transfer it to a blender and whiz with the ice for a softer, creamier taste.

If you feel a cold coming on, or your body's defenses are going down, have a glass of this vitamin C- and calcium-rich juice. It is green power in a glass.

**Nutritional Values**

Carbs 5.3 g ● Kcals 70 ● Vitamin C 143 mg ● Calcium 153 mg

**star low-carb**

# Red cabbage, grape, & orange juice

5 oz **red cabbage**

½ **orange**, peeled

⅓ cup **red grapes**

2–3 **ice cubes**

**orange slice,** to decorate

Makes ¾ cup

Separate the cabbage into leaves. Separate the orange into segments. Juice together the red cabbage, orange, and grapes then transfer the juice to a blender and whiz with a couple of ice cubes. Pour into a glass and decorate with an orange slice.

This juice is surprisingly sweet and if it is taken with a high-protein snack such as poached chicken or tuna, it can stabilize sugar cravings and maintain energy levels.

**Nutritional Values**

Carbs 13.5 g ● Kcals 64 ● Vitamin C 110 mg ● Calcium 116 mg

# Berry fizz

1 cup **mixed berries**

½ cup **sparkling mineral water**

2–3 **ice cubes**

Makes ¾ **cup**

Freeze the berries, then juice them and pour the juice into a jug. Mix with the sparkling water and serve over ice.

Berries are full of anthocyanides—phytonutrients that boost the immune system and keep the digestive system healthy.

**Nutritional Values**

Carbs 7.6 g ● Kcals 37 ● Vitamin C 22 mg ● Calcium 61.5 mg

# Index

# Acknowledgments

**Executive Editor:** Nicola Hill
**Project Editor:** Kate Tuckett
**Executive Art Editor:** Rozelle Bentheim
**Designer:** Ginny Zeal
**Production Controller:** Manjit Sihra
**Photographer:** Gareth Sambidge
**Food Stylist:** David Morgan

**OTHER PHOTOGRAPHY:**
**Octopus Publishing Group Limited**/Frank Adam 5 bottom center right, 18 bottom left, 19 center right, 48 center, 60 Top, 80 center, 92 center, 104 center; /Jeremy Hopley 16 top left, 18 center left bottom, 34 top, 124 top; /David Jordan 9 bottom center right, 16 center left bottom, 36 center, 58 top, 62 top; /Sandra Lane 80 Top, 88 center, 102 center, 108 Top, 114 Top; /Gary Latham 56 Top, 100 top; /William Lingwood 4, 5 center, 5 top right, 5 bottom right, 5 top center right, 6 top left, 6 bottom left, 7 top right, 8 center left, 10 top, 11 center right, 15 top right, 15 center right, 16 bottom left, 18 center left, 18 center left top, 19 bottom right, 19 center right bottom, 20 center left bottom, 21 bottom right, 21 top center right, 24 top, 24 center, 30 center, 32 center, 42 top, 42 center, 44 top, 46 top, 50 top, 50 center, 62 center, 64 center, 74 center, 76 top, 102 top, 108 center, 110 center, 112 top, 116 top, 120 top; /Ian O'Leary 9 top left; /Lis Parsons 8 top left, 16 center left top, 17 center right top, 21 center right, 26 top, 52 center, 58 center, 94, 94 center; /William Reavell 9 bottom left, 9 top center right, 10 center, 11 top right, 13 top, 14 top left, 14 center left, 17 bottom right, 20 center, 21 top right, 28 top, 28 center, 38 center, 44 center, 56 center, 60 center, 68 center, 74 top, 76 center, 88 top, 98 center, 104 top, 106 top, 114 center, 118 top, 118 center; /Simon Smith 7 center right, 9 top right; /Karen Thomas 17 center right bottom, 90 top, 112 center; /Ian Wallace 19 top right, 20 bottom left, 20 center left top, 26 center, 40 center, 54 center, 64 top, 66 top, 72 top, 106 center.
**Imagesource** 12 top left, 12 center left.